About the author, Ze'ev Zion:

I work professionally supporting America, Israel and the Jewish people. In the past I worked for influential Jewish and pro-Israel organizations. Unfortunately, too many fellow Jews, who mean well, don't believe in proudly defending Israel. As a result, young Jews are growing up and embracing values antithetical to Judaism. I was compelled to write this book in order to provide a way for our children to understand the facts about Israel, in an age appropriate manner, before they are exposed to the many antisemitic lies that pervade our society online, at school and in the media.

You can reach me at
Counterboycott1948@gmail.com

For my family. May Israel always be strong for the Jewish people.

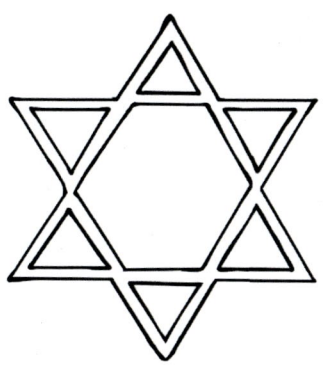

Z is for Zionism

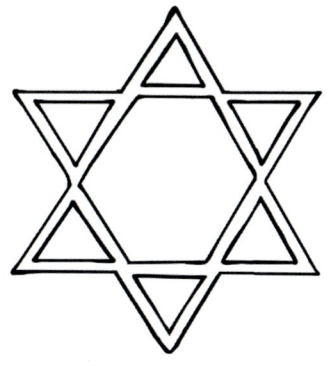

Thousands of years ago, the ruler of the universe, God, made a covenant with Abraham, the very first Jew. A covenant is like an agreement. God promised to give the land of Israel to the Jewish people. Later on, God gave his commandments, which are like rules, to the Jews in the Torah. It is these three things—God, Torah and Israel—that form the foundation of Judaism.

With help from the great Jewish leader, Moses, God told the Jews that he is the one and only God, it is important to be a good person, it is wrong to steal, and you should honor your father and mother, among other commandments. The Jews were chosen by God to spread this important message to help everyone around the world live a better life. This was a big deal!

But this made lots of people upset. Some didn't like that the Jews introduced God and moral demands into the world. Others told lies about Jews and blamed them for problems in society. While others didn't like that the Jews were different than them. This poor treatment of Jews is called antisemitism.

Eventually, because of antisemitism, Roman conquerors destroyed the Jewish people's prayer Temple and kicked most of them out of the land of Israel. Some Jews still remained.

For thousands of years, the land of Israel was conquered and ruled by many different groups, including the Romans, Muslims, Greeks and Turks. But none of them had the same historical, legal or God-given right to the land as the Jews. Also, they didn't have the same level of emotional attachment to the land as the Jews.

The Jews continued to be treated very poorly by many as they lived in other countries around the world. But no matter where they were, they always thought of their homeland and dreamed about returning.

Finally, in the 19th century-2,000 years after the Jews were originally kicked out of Israel -Theodor Herzl, Chaim Weizmann, Ze'ev Jabotinski and other Jewish leaders became tired of Jews being pushed around.

So they decided to figure out a way for the Jews to return home to the land of Israel to create a State where they could live in peace. This is what became known as *Zionism*. As a result, thousands of Jewish people started moving back to the land of Israel.

Then, in Europe in the middle of the twentieth century, the Nazis took control of Germany. The Nazis, led by an evil man named Hitler, were a group that hated Jews. The Nazis destroyed Jewish businesses, kicked Jews out of their homes, separated them from their families and forced them to live in concentration camps. Because of the Nazis evil regime, 6 million Jews lost their lives. It was the worst event in human history. This was the Holocaust.

After the Holocaust Jews swore that they would *Never Again* allow something like that to happen. The Holocaust reinforced why *Zionism* was so important. The Jewish people needed to return to Israel, not only because it belonged to them, but also so they could join together with one another and defend themselves.

Many world leaders agreed. The Zionist dream became a reality as the Jewish State of Israel declared its independence in 1948.

This caused an eruption of antisemitism in Arab countries where Jews had lived for thousands of years. Hundreds of thousands of Jews were kicked out of their homes and immediately found refuge in Israel.

Israel was then attacked by its surrounding Arab neighbors, Lebanon, Syria, Iraq, Jordan, and Egypt. Miraculously, Israel won the war. The people who thought creating a Jewish State would stop antisemitism were wrong. Many people who didn't like Jews also didn't like Israel because it was the Jewish state.

Also, because of Israel's small size and narrow borders, it was vulnerable to its enemies. Israel was constantly under attack.

In response, Israel developed a strong military in order to live up to the promise of

Never Again.

In 1967, Israel's brave soldiers liberated its capital city, Jerusalem, in a defensive war that took only six days. For so long, the Islamic occupiers of Jerusalem would not let Jews into the city. Finally, the Jews could pray at the Western Wall, the last remaining structure of their destroyed Temple. This was a significant moment in Jewish history.

But Israel's troubles were not over yet. The Palestinian Arabs, some of whom lived in Israel alongside the Jews, especially did not like Israel and tried very hard to kick the Jews out.

Israel tried to make peace over and over again with the Palestinian Arabs. Israel offered to share the land with them and even agreed to give up part of Israel to create a Palestinian state. But the Palestinian Arabs were not interested.

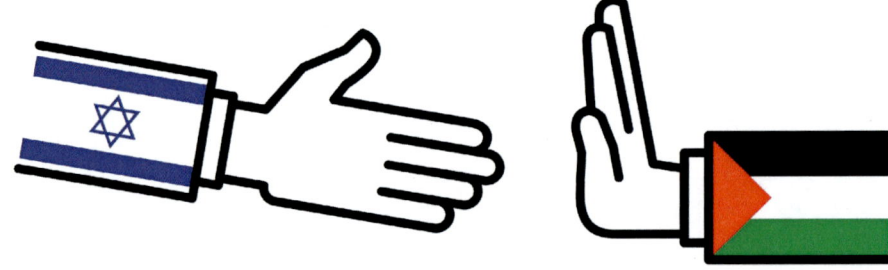

More than 70 years after the modern state of Israel was created, it still has many enemies.

But Israel does an excellent job defending itself. Israel has one of the most powerful militaries in the world. Israel is strong, smart, confident, successful and gives Jews all around the world pride. Israel is thriving.

In Israel, the Jewish people, from basically nothing, built up a wonderful society. They farmed the land, grew food and built cities like Tel Aviv, improving the lives of everyone who lived there and helping people around the world with amazing Israeli businesses and inventions.

TEL AVIV

Some examples of groundbreaking Israeli inventions are:

- Systems to make computers faster.
- Drip irrigation to help farmers grow food and save water.
- And the phone app, WAZE, which helps people driving find out how to get to their destination.

Also, Israeli doctors invented new medicines to help people when they're sick. For example, a tiny pill that contains a camera that can detect cancer when swallowed was invented in Israel!

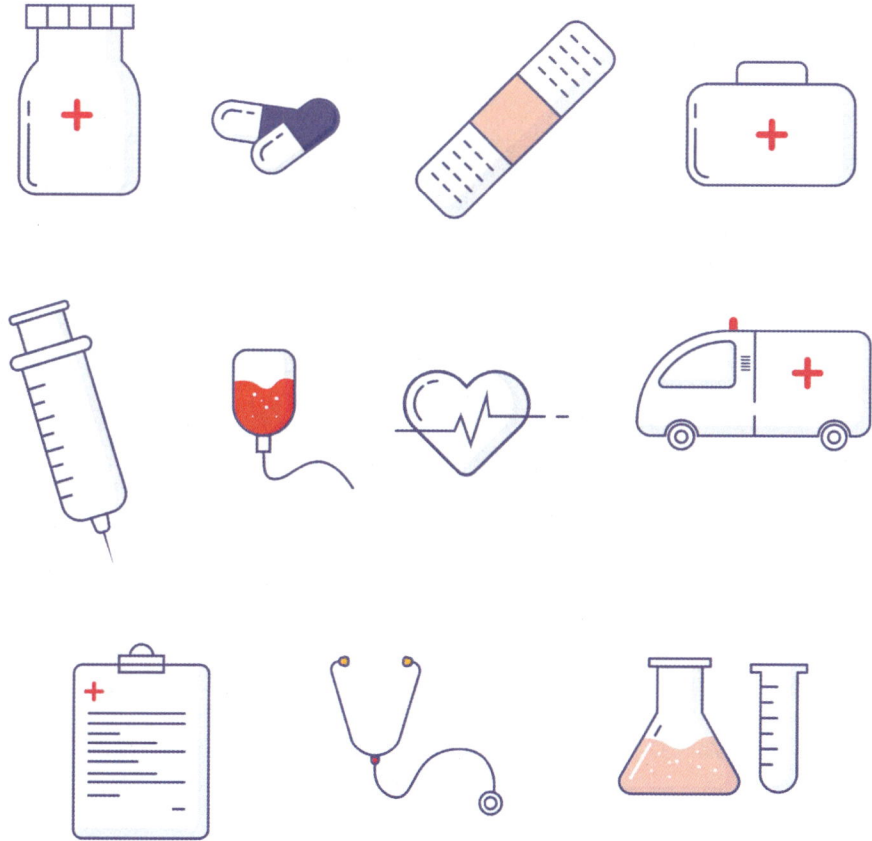

Israel is a generous country. It has welcomed in poor and struggling Jewish people from all over the world. When the Soviet Union was oppressing Jews, Israel opened its door to 1 million of them who found safety, freedom and dignity in Israel.

Israel is a free country that treats all of its citizens fairly, even the ones that aren't Jewish. Israel is the only country in the Middle East that truly lets its citizens choose who leads them. This is called democracy.

Israel is home to terrific schools where people from different backgrounds learn. Some of the smartest students in the world study at Israeli universities. They study science, math, history, engineering, Hebrew and medicine.

When there are serious problems around the world, like hurricanes or earthquakes, Israel sends over experts to help. When there was a devastating earthquake in Haiti, Israel was one of the first countries to send crews to treat the injured and clean up the destruction.

Israel and the United States have a special relationship. This is partly due to the large Christian community in the United States that is very supportive of Israel. The two countries share information and technology and work together to help keep the world safe.

Israel is now home to millions of Jews and lots of other different types of people, including Christians and Muslims.

A strong Israel will ensure the future of the Jewish people. Jews around the world know that they have a home they can visit or even move to one day if they want. The *Zionist* dream has become a reality. Be a proud *Zionist*. Maybe one day, you will visit Israel.

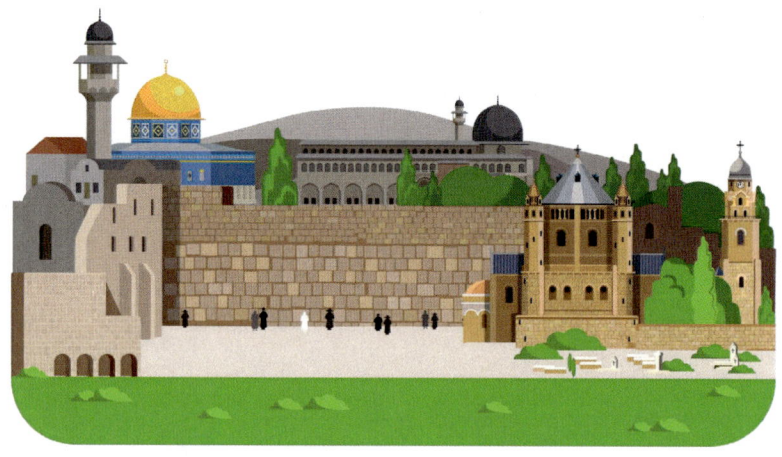

Dreamstime Illustration credits:

- © Anna Hirna | Dreamstime.com
- © Luis Carlos Torres | Dreamstime.com
- © Onyxprj | Dreamstime.com
- © Bisli | Dreamstime.com
- © Anna Pindyurina | Dreamstime.com
- © Pytyczech | Dreamstime.com
- © Brushpiquetr | Dreamstime.com
- © Ayeletkeshet | Dreamstime.com
- © Thelittleprince3 | Dreamstime.com
- © Oleksandr Bolotov | Dreamstime.com
- © Maxim Popov | Dreamstime.com
- © Ernest Akayeu | Dreamstime.com
- © ValenZi17 | Dreamstime.com
- © Sentavio | Dreamstime.com
- © Dennis Crow | Dreamstime.com
- © Martin Malchev | Dreamstime.com
- © Linda Bucklin | Dreamstime.com
- © David Carillet | Dreamstime.com
- © Mast3r | Dreamstime.com
- © Martin Malchev | Dreamstime.com
- © Anastasia Ispuganova | Dreamstime.com
- © Sergeypykhonin | Dreamstime.com
- © Ominaesi | Dreamstime.com
- © Molotok007 | Dreamstime.com
- © Brushpiquetr | Dreamstime.com
- © Doomko | Dreamstime.com
- © Olesia Sarycheva | Dreamstime.com
- © Stokio | Dreamstime.com
- © Tashatuvango | Dreamstime.com
- © Alexandr Petukhov | Dreamstime.com
- © Robot100 | Dreamstime.com
- © Pavel Mastepanov | Dreamstime.com
- © Petrovv | Dreamstime.com
- © Rudiestrummer | Dreamstime.com
- © Alexlmx | Dreamstime.com
- © Sprinter81 | Dreamstime.com
- © Bolid2000 | Dreamstime.com
- © Anton Medvedev | Dreamstime.com

Test your child on what they learned:

1.) Who was the very first Jew?
2.) What is anti-semitism?
3.) What three things form the foundation of Judaism?
4.) After the Holocaust, what did the Jews promise?
5.) When did Israel declare its independence?
6.) Why is Israel so important for the Jewish people?
7.) What are some of Israel's achievements?
8.) Who refuses to make peace with Israel?
9.) With which country does Israel have a special relationship?

Learn more...

For more detailed information on Jewish and Israel history, please visit the *Jewish Virtual Library* online. Also, as your child grows older, here are some great pro-Israel organizations for them to get involved in:
- Club Z: Clubz.org
  - Organization that educates high school students about Israel and the Middle East.
- ZOA: ZOA.org
  - One of the oldest pro-Israel organizations in America.
- Stand with Us: Standwithus.com
  - Trains college students to defend Israel.
- SSI: SSImovement.org
  - Pro-Israel student group in college.
- Prager U: Prageru.com
  - Educates young adults with short videos about traditional American values, which includes supporting Israel.

Answers to questions:
1.) Abraham
2.) The poor treatment of Jews
3.) God, Israel, Torah
4.) Never Again
5.) 1948
6.) Because God gave it to them, it is their home, it provides Jews with safety and security, and it ensures the Jewish future
7.) Taking in struggling Jews; inventions that help people; being the only democracy in the Middle East; helping other countries in need
8.) Palestinian Arabs
9.) United States